HOW TO BE
KIND

I would like to thank everyone who shared their personal stories of kindness for this book. Each gesture clearly had a big impact on the individual, with some acts of kindness remembered for many years after the event.

We have changed the names of all contributors to preserve their anonymity.

Cara Frost-Sharratt

An Hachette UK Company
www.hachette.co.uk

First published in 2015 by Bounty Books,
a division of Octopus Publishing Group Ltd
Carmelite House
50 Victoria Embankment
London, EC4Y 0DZ

www.octopusbooks.co.uk

ISBN: 978-0-7537-2966-3

A CIP catalogue record for this book is available from the British Library

Printed and bound in China

10 9 8 7 6 5 4 3 2 1

Design: Wide Open Design
Publisher: Samantha Warrington
Art director: Miranda Snow
Managing editor: Karen Rigden
Editor: Phoebe Morgan
Production controller: Meskerem Berhane

Picture Credits

Shutterstock :
Africa Studio 74; Andrekart Photography 66; Arthur Hidden 60; Balazs Kovacs Images 30, 40; Brandon Bourdages 70; Dean Fikar 77; DeepGreen 57; Elena Stepanova 13; Frank Fischbach 69; IgorAleks 21; Kamil Macniak 28; katarinag 5; Kunal Mehta 32; Milosz_G 47; misfire_asia 64; Rawpixel 41; Skreidzeleu 24; StevanZZ 11; Vibrant Image Studio 17, 82; Zagorodnaya 14; Zurijeta 44.

HOW TO BE
KIND

TALES OF INSPIRATION
AND LESSONS IN KINDNESS

CARA FROST-SHARRATT

Bounty
Books

INTRODUCTION

Human beings have a natural tendency towards kindness and protection. This helps to partly explain our survival and longevity on the planet – by working together and helping those less fortunate or able, we have ensured our success as a species. Although it sometimes seems that the world is full of cruelty and inhumanity, we should remember that the reason these stories are so shocking is that they go against most people's natural instincts.

From simple gestures – such as helping a parent lift a stroller up a flight of steps, giving blood, or coming to the aid of a child who has fallen over, to instinctive selfless acts like running into a burning building to save someone's life, our urge to help and protect our fellow humans seems inbuilt and instinctive.

The golden rule

Altruism – or selflessness – is as old as humanity and the basic principle of kindness has woven itself into the cornerstones of all cultures and organized religions, as an ethical code for people to live their lives by. Often referred to as the "Golden Rule", it varies slightly between religions but the basic message is simple – treat others as you yourself would like to be treated.

Kindness in the modern world

Modern life can be busy and stressful, and it doesn't always work harmoniously with the Golden Rule. Whether at work or at home with the family, it can be easy to slip into bad habits, take people for granted and just assume things will get done. But our daily interactions with other people can have a massive impact on our mood and sense of wellbeing. That's why it's important to take a step back every so often and reflect on the way you treat other people. That doesn't mean you have to go soul searching; just take a moment to appreciate the things that matter the most.

The smallest action or reaction can alter the course of a person's day, and if everyone aimed for one daily act of kindness, just think of the combined effect on humanity's mood. Did the parking attendant give you a ticket, or let you off with a kind warning? Did you get annoyed with your son when he spilled the milk at breakfast, or did you tell him that accidents happen, and help him to mop it up? Did you ignore the homeless person on the sidewalk or did you stop and give them a few coins or a friendly word?

The science of kindness

Aside from the feel-good factor and the knowledge of giving someone else a small slice of happiness, the positive effects of kindness are also backed up by science. Research has found that altruistic behavior can increase your happiness levels. Endorphins or 'happy chemicals' are produced in the brain following acts of kindness and psychologists have coined the phrase "helper's high" to describe the feelings of

euphoria and subsequent calmness that altruism creates. Being kind can also release the hormone oxytocin. Sometimes called the 'bonding' hormone, oxytocin helps to keep stress levels down and can induce feelings of calm and happiness.

The knock-on effect

Good deeds come in all shapes and sizes and you'll find a collection of real-life stories from around the world and throughout history in this book. These tales sit alongside inspirational quotes and simple ideas of how you can bring a little kindness into your life and the lives of others. On the next page is a little guide to what you'll find inside.

Kindness lives long in people's memories and the powerful impact of good deeds are often felt long after the event itself, with a simple act of kindness starting a domino effect. So, what good deed will you do today?

THE KINDNESS OF STRANGERS

These real-life stories demonstrate the natural instinct of human beings to comfort and care for each other and to help out in times of need. From the smallest gesture to the greatest personal sacrifice, each act of kindness has left a permanent imprint on the recipient and, in many cases, led to other good deeds.

BE KIND FOR LIFE

Kindness shouldn't be a one-off gesture, it should be a mantra for life – something that becomes a natural and regular part of your daily activities. If you build positive acts into the fabric of your life, they will soon become second nature. You might have time to spare that could be put to good use helping others, or you might decide that some of your salary could be better spent on good causes. These are ideas for ongoing acts of kindness that could have a huge impact on the people and environment around you.

KINDNESS THROUGH THE AGES

History is full of incredible stories of kindness – people putting their safety and lives at risk in order to help and save others. Be inspired by these tales of kind acts that cross countries and centuries.

DAILY ACTS OF KINDNESS

You don't need to spend a lot of time or money to make a big difference to someone else's day – sometimes the smallest gestures can have a lasting impact. Kindness can break down barriers, heal ills, change moods, avert arguments and build bridges across social and cultural divides – after all, you don't need to speak the same language to pick up a dropped purse or smile at a stranger.

WORDS OF WISDWOM

Kindness is a human trait that we admire, appreciate and aspire to. The good deeds of others are often inspirational and these quotes, thoughts and proverbs demonstrate the rich emotional links that human beings have with kind gestures.

TICKET TO RIDE

I was about to catch the train home
from work when I saw a girl of about 14
in tears. She'd lost her ticket and the man at
the ticket office had refused to issue a
replacement. I bought her a new one –
it wasn't much money but I figured
that it could so easily have been
my little sister and I'd hope that
someone would do the
same for her.

Taylor M

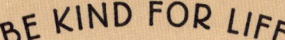

Voluntary work

Whether it's your local animal shelter, women's refuge, food bank or thrift store, there are endless causes that rely on the goodwill of others in order to continue their work. Time is precious and any time you can give up on a regular basis will be greatly appreciated.

Sponsor a child

There are a number of charities that give donors the opportunity to sponsor a child or family living in poverty. Your monthly contribution will be spent on the whole community but you have the opportunity to build up a relationship with your sponsor family through letters, cards and photos.

Charity swap

How many times have you received unwanted gifts from your relatives? Each holiday you smile enthusiastically then tuck the socks/board game/ cheese knives in a drawer and forget about them. Wouldn't it be nicer to see the money spent on good causes? Make a pact with your family to donate the money you would have spent on presents to a chosen charity instead – you could take turns choosing the charity each year.

Call a friend or family member who you haven't spoken to for a long time, or have lost contact with.

Donate some items from your grocery shop to a food bank – many stores now have a dedicated box or collection area after the checkout.

HURRICANE HERO

The American Can Company is a residential building in New Orleans. In the aftermath of Hurricane Katrina, resident John Keller almost single-handedly ensured the safety and survival of the 170 people who had remained in their apartments when the storm struck – many of them elderly and disabled. The floodwaters had taken over the lobby, cutting the building off, but instead of jumping in a boat and rowing himself to safety, John chose to stay and protect the vulnerable residents. As an ex-Marine he had the training and stamina to take on the role of guardian and he kept his wits about him as he saw off intruders and looters, and swam to get food and medicine for residents. John then helped to evacuate every last person from the building – using an air mattress, a hot-wired boat and sheer strength to carry wheelchair-bound residents to waiting helicopters.

A PRESENT FOR A PASSERBY

Last year I was walking along a street I'd never been to before. I came upon a trestle table laden with new, boxed sets of make up (still in their packaging) outside someone's driveway.

Also on the table was a notebook and pen, laid out next to a handwritten sign. The sign said: "Please take an item. All free and brand new. If you have time, please write in the book to say why you took an item and how this made you feel. There is no catch. I just want to do something nice for niceness's sake."

I took a small item and wrote: "I stumbled upon this with pleasant surprise and felt this was a really serene gesture. I will find something to do to pass it on." I now volunteer once a week for a charity-funded playgroup and I often think of this unknown person.

Sara F.

"To be rich in admiration and free from envy, to rejoice greatly in the good of others, to love with such generosity of heart that your love is still a dear possession in absence or unkindness – these are the gifts which money cannot buy."

Robert Louis Stevenson (1850-1894)

Have a friend's kids for a sleepover or offer to babysit for the evening so your friend can have a much-needed night out.

Give up your seat on the bus for someone who looks tired (but don't tell them they look tired!)

"What wisdom can
you find that is greater
than kindness?"

Jean-Jacques Rousseau (1712–1778)

"You have not lived until you
have done something for someone
who can never repay you."

Anonymous

Plant a tree

Trees can live for many years and they make a
positive contribution to the environment. If you don't
have space in your garden for a large tree, offer to
pay for one to be planted in your local park. Better
still, gather some friends together and have a "tree
planting" party – if everyone donated a little time
and money you could plant a small orchard.

THE LAST LIFE BELT

High-society gentleman Alfred Vanderbilt was a passenger on board the RMS Lusitania when a German torpedo hit and sank the ship in 1915. Alfred handed out life belts to other passengers and then gave his own to a young mother who was carrying a baby. In the process of doing so, as Alfred couldn't swim, he sacrificed his own life. In a strange twist of irony, it turned out that Alfred had cancelled his own passage on the fateful Titanic voyage just three years earlier in 1912.

"I feel that there is nothing more truly artistic than to love people."

Vincent Van Gogh (1853–1890)

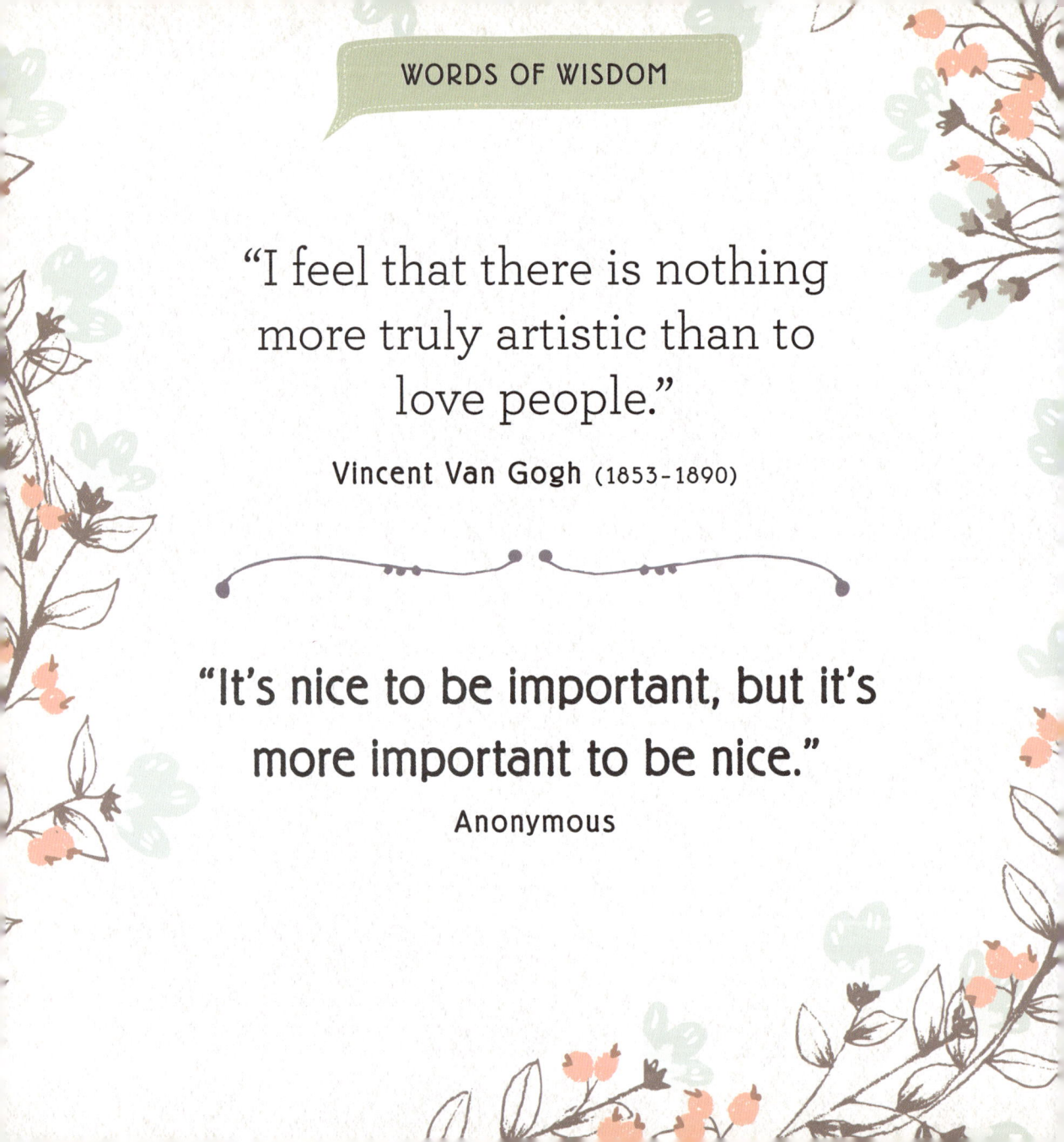

"It's nice to be important, but it's more important to be nice."

Anonymous

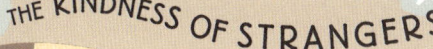
CHANGING ATTITUDES

I grew up in a small village in Ireland and my grandaunt Dooney lived with us and helped my mother look after the five children. Dooney was well respected in the community, so when there was talk of a local woman giving birth to an illegitimate child she was among the first to know. This was a big deal in Ireland 50 years ago and the woman was shunned. She would sit outside church on a Sunday, afraid that no one would sit near her if she went inside. Dooney spoke to her one day, inviting her to stop by our house the following week so they could walk to church together. Sure enough, as the congregation settled into their seats that Sunday, Dooney strolled to the front pew, arm-in-arm with the woman. If Dooney accepted her and her child, so would the rest of the community.

Shaun C.

Offer to go shopping
for an elderly neighbor or
a friend who is sick and
can't get out of the house.

Offer the refuse
collector a cup of coffee
when they're next
cleaning your street.

Pay for two rounds of drinks
in a row on a night out.

"I expect to pass through life but once. If, therefore, there be any kindness I can show, or any good I can do to any fellow being, let me do it now, and not defer or neglect it, as I shall not pass this way again."

William Penn (1644-1718)

Back to school

School board members fill a vital role in communicating between parents and teachers in schools. They hold great sway in important decisions and give their time on a voluntary basis. You don't have to have a child attending the school to become a member but you might have links to the school or simply want to make a difference.

Become a foster parent

This is obviously not something you can do on a whim – it takes a great deal of time and commitment to go through the process to become a foster parent but it is one of the greatest gifts you can give a child. So many children need a safe and nurturing environment while they are waiting to be adopted.

Donor card

The gift of life is the ultimate act of kindness – by registering for an organ donation card you are offering this gift to a stranger, should anything untoward happen to you. You never know who might be grateful.

Give your kids' teacher or child-minder a box of chocolates as a thank you for all their hard work.

Send a letter, postcard or relevant newspaper clipping to a friend – we're spoilt with technology these days but nothing beats finding a handwritten envelope in the mailbox.

TACKLING ANTARCTICA

Ernest Henry Shackleton was a seasoned Antarctic explorer, but his most famous expedition took place between 1914 and 1916, when he made his third trip to the continent in the aptly named *Endurance*. Partway through the expedition, the ship became firmly wedged in the ice.

Before it sank, the ship crew abandoned it and set up camp in tents on the drifting ice. With no means of contacting the outside world, they used lifeboats to try and reach a safer position. The men eventually spotted Elephant Island, almost 500 days since they had last stepped foot on land.

They were safe but no-one knew their location, and they were off course for any passing ships. Someone would have to sail to the nearest inhabitation, which was over 800 miles away at South Georgia. Shackleton and five other men took 16 days to make the treacherous crossing.

Eventually, Shackleton's party made their way to a whaling station to get help, and the stranded men were rescued after 137 days on the island. The fact that every member of the exhibition survived is testament to Shackleton's leadership skills, bravery and determination to save every man.

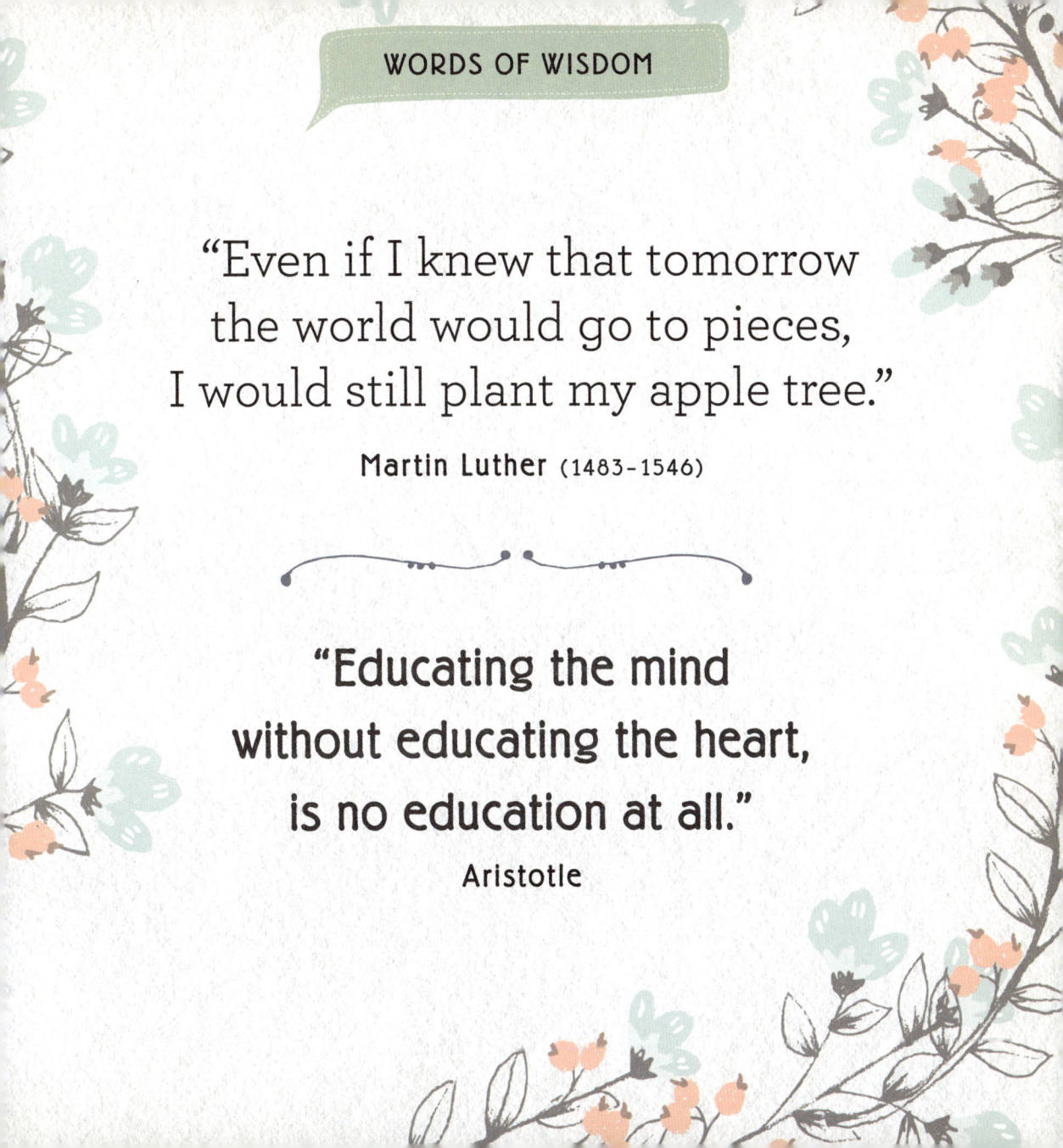

"Even if I knew that tomorrow
the world would go to pieces,
I would still plant my apple tree."

Martin Luther (1483–1546)

"Educating the mind
without educating the heart,
is no education at all."

Aristotle

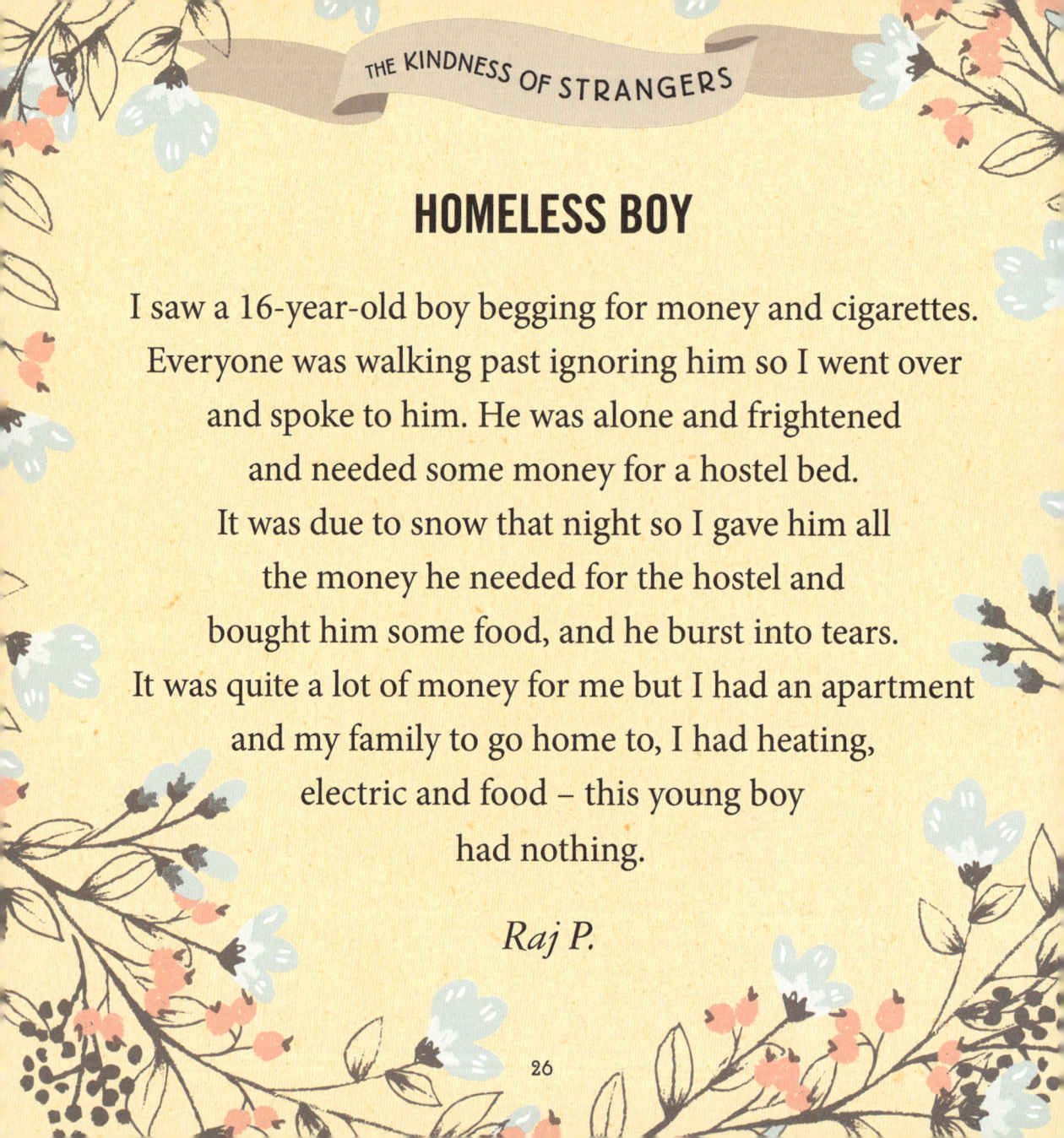

HOMELESS BOY

I saw a 16-year-old boy begging for money and cigarettes.
Everyone was walking past ignoring him so I went over
and spoke to him. He was alone and frightened
and needed some money for a hostel bed.
It was due to snow that night so I gave him all
the money he needed for the hostel and
bought him some food, and he burst into tears.
It was quite a lot of money for me but I had an apartment
and my family to go home to, I had heating,
electric and food – this young boy
had nothing.

Raj P.

Organize an annual event

Do you enjoy organizing events? How about setting up an annual coffee morning, quiz or garden party for a local good cause? If you choose a specific date each year you'll have plenty of time for planning and getting other people involved.

Be a bone marrow donor

This is something you can do that will have a life-long impact on a stranger. The sooner you register, the more likelihood there is of you being a match for someone one day. Although donation requires a number of visits to hospital, the process is fairly quick and your donation could help to treat somebody with a condition like lymphoma or leukemia.

Buy your spouse a bunch of flowers for no particular reason.

Leave a book or magazine that you have finished reading on the train or bus, with a note saying "enjoy".

A BASKET OF KINDNESS

My sister was in a supermarket one holiday
when she overheard a mother telling her children that the
family didn't have enough money to buy the festive treats
they wanted. The children looked disappointed but seemed to
understand and the woman carefully selected
the basics her budget could stretch to. My sister
filled a basket with Christmas goodies –
desserts, crackers, candies and meat. She then
paid for the groceries and waited for the woman
to finish shopping. She handed her the bags
of shopping and wished her and her
children a Happy Holiday.

Anouska M.

Take a homemade cake or one-pot dinner to an elderly neighbor – the gesture will be appreciated as much for the contact and conversation as for the food itself.

Run for kindness

If you enjoy running, why not make
a pledge to yourself to compete in a
marathon or half marathon each year
to raise money for a different charity?
People are always happy to donate
for such a mammoth feat of endurance.

Get back to nature

If you're looking for an investment
for some savings, why not buy an area
of woodland instead and protect this
precious resource for generations to come?
It's a wonderful way to reintroduce
children to nature and outdoor crafts
and, as owner of the woodland, you
are its custodian.

"The smallest act of kindness is
worth more than the greatest intention."

Oscar Wilde (1854–1900)

THE VANISHING RESCUER

A number of stories of heroism and selflessness emerged after 9/11 but one stands out in particular. Jason Thomas, a retired US Marine, was 30 miles from Ground Zero when the first plane hit the tower. He dusted off his Marine uniform and drove directly to the scene of the attack with the sole purpose of trying to help rescue people. Once there, he joined another volunteer and they set about searching the debris for survivors. During the night, they heard voices coming from below. Together they managed to pull free two seriously injured police officers – men who would almost certainly have died if the volunteers hadn't persisted in their efforts.

Jason Thomas left the scene after the rescue – he had accomplished his mission and didn't want to be recognized for bravery or be reminded of the horrors he witnessed that day. He remained anonymous for five years but when he saw a trailer for the film *World Trade Center* – based on the story of the two policemen – Jason saw his role in their rescue play out on screen and knew it was time to come forward. The policemen were two of only 20 survivors who were freed from the wreckage of the World Trade Center.

WRONG NUMBER

Last year I took my two daughters to Spain. I was really nervous, as it was our first vacation abroad. When we arrived at the airport I tried calling my friend who we were staying with, but the call wouldn't connect and kept saying "incorrect number". I had no other way of contacting her and I was on the verge of tears when an old Italian lady who spoke no English offered me her cell to try. The number still didn't work but the lady stayed with me, as I was really upset. Then a Nigerian man came over and helped me look up my friend's number on his laptop. We eventually found it and I managed to contact my friend. I was amazed at the kindness of two complete strangers from different parts of the world stopping to help a single mother having a panic in a foreign airport. I hugged them both.

Laura G.

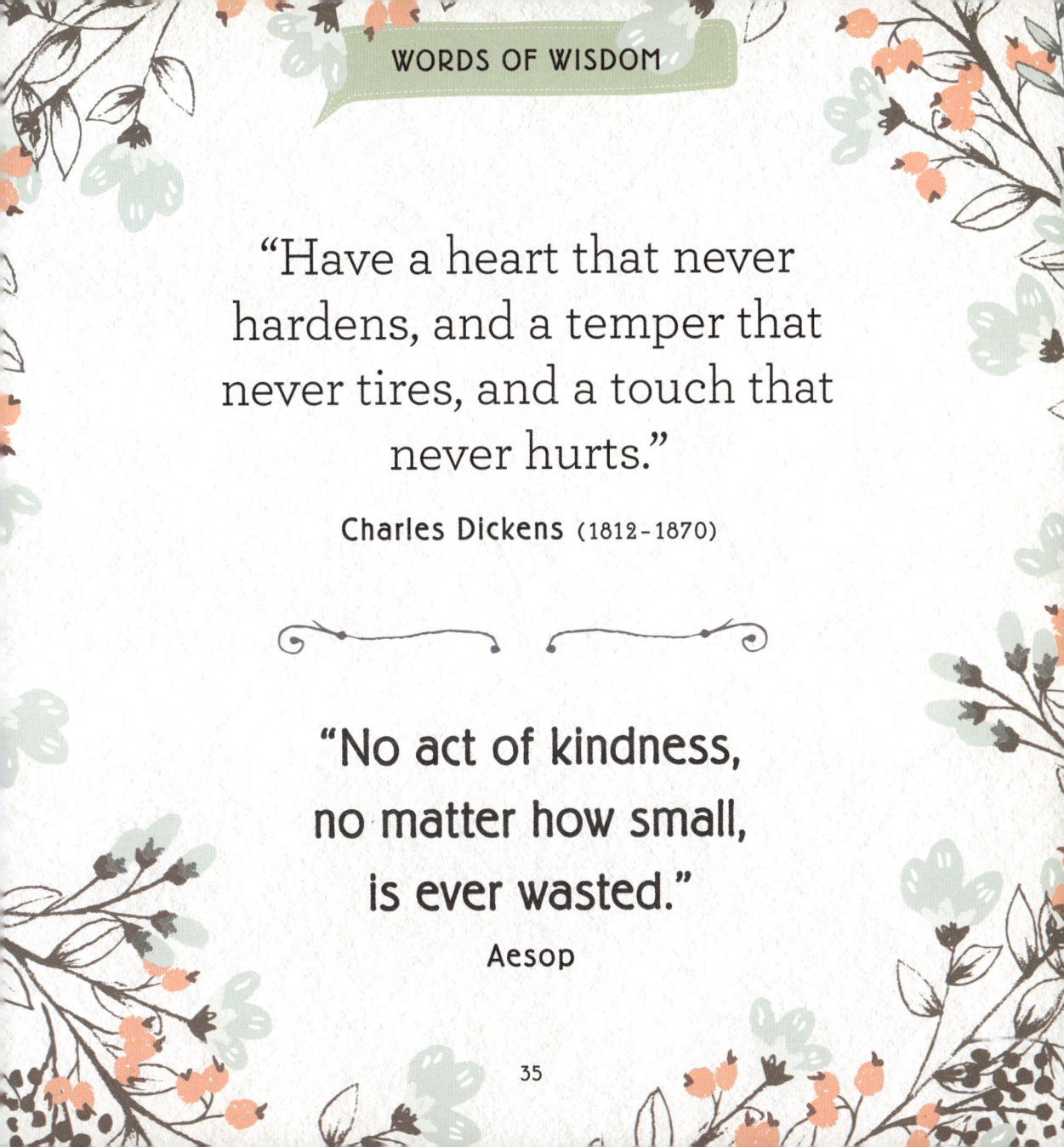

"Have a heart that never hardens, and a temper that never tires, and a touch that never hurts."

Charles Dickens (1812–1870)

"No act of kindness, no matter how small, is ever wasted."

Aesop

Environmental kindness

The way we live now will have a huge impact on the world that future generations inhabit. By making small changes to our lives, we can help conserve valuable natural resources and protect vulnerable ecosystems, as well as the people and animals living there. Think about the car you drive, the amount you use it, the effort you make with recycling and the number of flights you take ... it all adds up.

Coach a team

If you're a keen sportsperson, you could offer your skills to a local team or after-school program. Sport is a great way for kids to stay fit, build social skills and stay out of trouble so your time will make a huge difference.

If you're traveling alone, move seats on the plane so a couple or family can sit together.

Hold the door open and smile for everyone you meet today.

Pay for the coffee of the person behind you in the line.

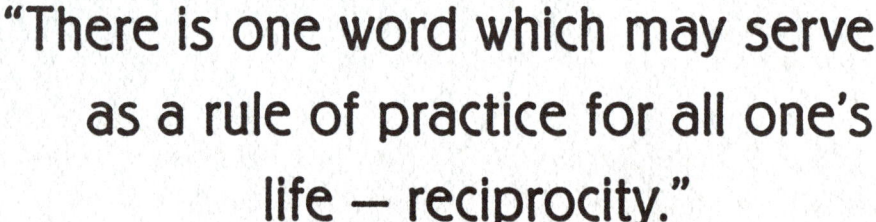

"There is one word which may serve as a rule of practice for all one's life — reciprocity."

Vincent Van Gogh (1853-1890)

"The greatest wisdom of all is kindness."

Hebrew

LOCKED OUT

I was on my balcony one day when I saw
an old lady at the block opposite struggling to
unlock her front door. I watched her for a little while
and debated whether I should offer to help – I didn't want her
to possibly think I was going to rob her or hurt her.
After a couple more minutes I ran down to
help and it turned out she had a new lock
fitted that was stiff. I managed to get her back
into her home and felt great that I could help,
as she is disabled and would have had
a long wait for her husband
to get home.

Milo H.

Help a lost tourist find their way – people are sometimes nervous about asking for help but will appreciate it if you offer.

"Three things in human life are important:
the first is to be kind; the second is to be kind;
and the third is to be kind."

Henry James (1843-1916)

THE HONORABLE FIGHTER PILOT

War demonstrates the extremes of human actions and emotions and the story of Charlie Brown and Franz Stigler is a good example. Following an aerial attack by a number of German bombers, American pilot Charlie Brown was unconscious and his plane had just one functioning engine.

As he came round and discovered that most of his crew was also seriously injured, he thought he had no chance of survival flying a stricken plane across German territory. It was then that he noticed a German plane flying alongside his, and he could see the pilot gesturing to him. It was impossible to understand what he was trying to say as he flew his plane alongside Charlie's.

Still in shock from the attack, Charlie wasn't sure what was happening but when the pilot saluted him, he knew instantly that he was being allowed to live, rather than being shot from the sky. In fact, Franz Stigler had come close to pulling the trigger – spurred on by the fact that one more successful mission would see him being awarded the Knight's Cross, which was the highest award bestowed by the German army in World War II. However, when he saw the plight of Charlie Brown and his crew, incapable of fighting back and having suffered incredible damage to the plane and personal injury, his sense of honor overcame his fighter's instinct. Franz helped to guide the plane out of enemy territory, peeling away just before he came into view of German gunners, who would almost certainly have shot down his plane if they had realized what he was doing.

The two men made contact many years later through a newspaper advertisement and they were finally able to meet face to face.

"Taking the first footstep with a good thought, the second with a good word and the third with a good deed I entered paradise."

Zoroaster

"One of the most difficult things to give away is kindness; usually it comes back to you."

Anonymous

THE CHILDREN'S HERO

In 1866 the 17-year-old Thomas Barnardo moved from Dublin to London, to train as a doctor and pursue his dream of becoming a missionary. But after spending time in the East End, Thomas abandoned his plans to emigrate in order to help deprived London children get the chance of an education. A cholera outbreak had left many children orphaned and in severe poverty, and Victorian London had little to offer them apart from the workhouse.

Thomas established the Ragged School but soon realized that many of the children needed more than an education; their primary need was food and shelter.

So, he opened a home for boys in 1870 and he made sure they would all be taught useful skills that would help them get jobs. A girls' home followed soon after and he stuck to his mantra of never turning away a destitute child.

Thomas Barnardo died in 1905 and his legacy was 96 children's homes that looked after almost 9,000 children. Today, the charity that he set up continues his inspirational work.

Pick up the loose garbage on your street, outside work, or outside your kids' school.

Donate blood at your local blood bank.

Ask a new colleague at work to join your table for lunch so they can meet other people in the office.

ANONYMOUS ORGAN DONATION

About four years ago I heard about altruistic kidney donation (donating a kidney to a stranger, rather than to a relative or friend). A distant relative was seriously ill with kidney disease at the time and his wife wanted to donate her kidney to him. Sadly, she wasn't a match but she was able to donate to a stranger and through a sequence of donations, my relative was matched with a suitable kidney. This got me thinking and I contacted a transplant center that performs many of these operations to begin the process.

I had to go through 11 months of rigorous medical and psychological testing, the most crucial being to test individual kidney function – in other words, checking that both kidneys function almost equally so that both the donor organ and the remaining kidney can do their jobs independently.

My kidney was removed by hand-assisted keyhole surgery, during a two-and-a-half hour operation. I spent five days in hospital and I have a three-inch scar just below my ribs. I was told that the kidney was implanted the same day into a 41-year-old man who had been on dialysis for eight years. I will probably never hear from him but I wish him well.

Ayla F.

DYING FOR THE FREEDOM OF OTHERS

Edith Cavell is one of the unsung heroines of World War I. A British nurse who worked in a clinic in German-occupied Belgium, Edith treated soldiers from both allied and German forces. She also helped to smuggle allied soldiers from Belgium into the neutral Netherlands so that they wouldn't be captured by the enemy. Edith paid the highest price for her selflessness. In 1915, she was arrested and during interrogation she confessed to her activities in the belief that she would save her colleagues from retribution. Edith was found guilty and sentenced to death.

"A kind word is like a spring day."

Russian

"He who sows courtesy reaps friendship, and he who plants kindness gathers love."

Spanish

"Write injuries in dust, but kindness in marble."

French

"Help your neighbor's boat across, and lo! your own has reached the shore."

Hindu

Say "thank you" to the bus driver to show your appreciation.

If someone is a few coins short for their groceries, lunch or drink, give them the difference so they don't have to leave empty handed.

FESTIVE GOODWILL

After suffering a devastating illness a few years ago, we were getting support from an organization. On Christmas Eve there was a knock on the door and we opened it to find a family of strangers who presented us with a huge festive hamper, complete with turkey, chocolates, wine, veg, fruit and cakes. It turned out that this family had previously been helped by the same organization and they wanted to give something back to show their appreciation. We were blown away and it made it the best holiday ever!

Stefan G.

"In hours of weariness, sensations sweet,
Felt in the blood, and felt along the heart;
And passing even into my purer mind,
With tranquil restoration: – feelings too,
Or unremembered pleasure: such, perhaps,
As have no slight or trivial influence
On that best portion of a good man's life,
His little, nameless, unremembered acts
Of kindness and of love …"

William Wordsworth (1770–1850)

DARLING OF THE SEAS

Grace Darling was the daughter of the lighthouse keeper on the Farne Islands in Northumberland. As a teenager, she frequently took to the seas with her father in dangerous conditions in a rowing boat to try and save shipwreck survivors. However, her name is most often linked to the 1838 Forfarshire rescue. During the night of September 7 1838, the steamer hit rocks during a storm and broke in half with 60 passengers and crew on board. Nine survivors managed to clamber onto the rocks but the rest perished in the sea. Watching the horror unfold from the lighthouse, 26-year-old Grace and her father immediately took their boat out and rowed over a mile into the choppy seas, ignoring their own safety in their quest to save lives. They managed to save all nine stranded passengers and bring them back to the lighthouse.

"Kindnesses, like grain,
increase by sowing."

German

"Better to light one small candle
than to curse the darkness."

Chinese

THE PURSE DETECTIVE

I was running down the platform to catch my train when my wallet flew out of my bag. I'd forgotten to do the zip up and I didn't notice until I was halfway home at which point I started panicking. Luckily I needn't have worried – a lady had found the wallet and managed to track me down via my dad and left a message so that by the time I reached home late that night, I knew my wallet was safe.

She returned the wallet to my husband in London the next day, telling him that as soon as she saw it lying on the platform she knew she had to make sure it got back to me safely as: "Your wife's life was in there and I've lost my purse a few times in the past." How right she was. A week later I'm still completely in awe that someone would go to that much effort for a complete stranger.

Mae Y

Let someone out at each
junction on your drive
to work today.

Buy a hot drink
and a sandwich for a
homeless person.

Pay the drinks bill
on a meal out with
family or a
group of friends.

"By being grateful, a man makes himself deserving of yet another kindness."

Nigerian

"Do not forget little kindnesses and do not remember small faults."

Chinese

"By good nature and kindness even fierce spirits become tractable."

Latin

"Kindness begets kindness."

Greek

Help a neighbor fix their car, move heavy boxes, sort out their garden
– just be observant and pitch in when someone needs a hand.

ACTING ON IMPULSE

Recently my 4-year-old daughter stopped suddenly
in the middle of the street and was sick at the side of the road.
I was holding her hair and trying to reassure her when a teenage
girl came over and asked if we needed help. I thanked her and
said we'd be fine but she went off and came back a few minutes
later with tissues and a bottle of chilled water from the corner
store across the street. She wouldn't accept any money for them.
She could not have been kinder and I was so grateful.

Charlotte E.

HAVE A TREAT ON ME

I found an envelope containing some money
taped to the vending machine at the train station.
Someone had left if there and written:
"Have a free treat on me," on it.

Saeed J.

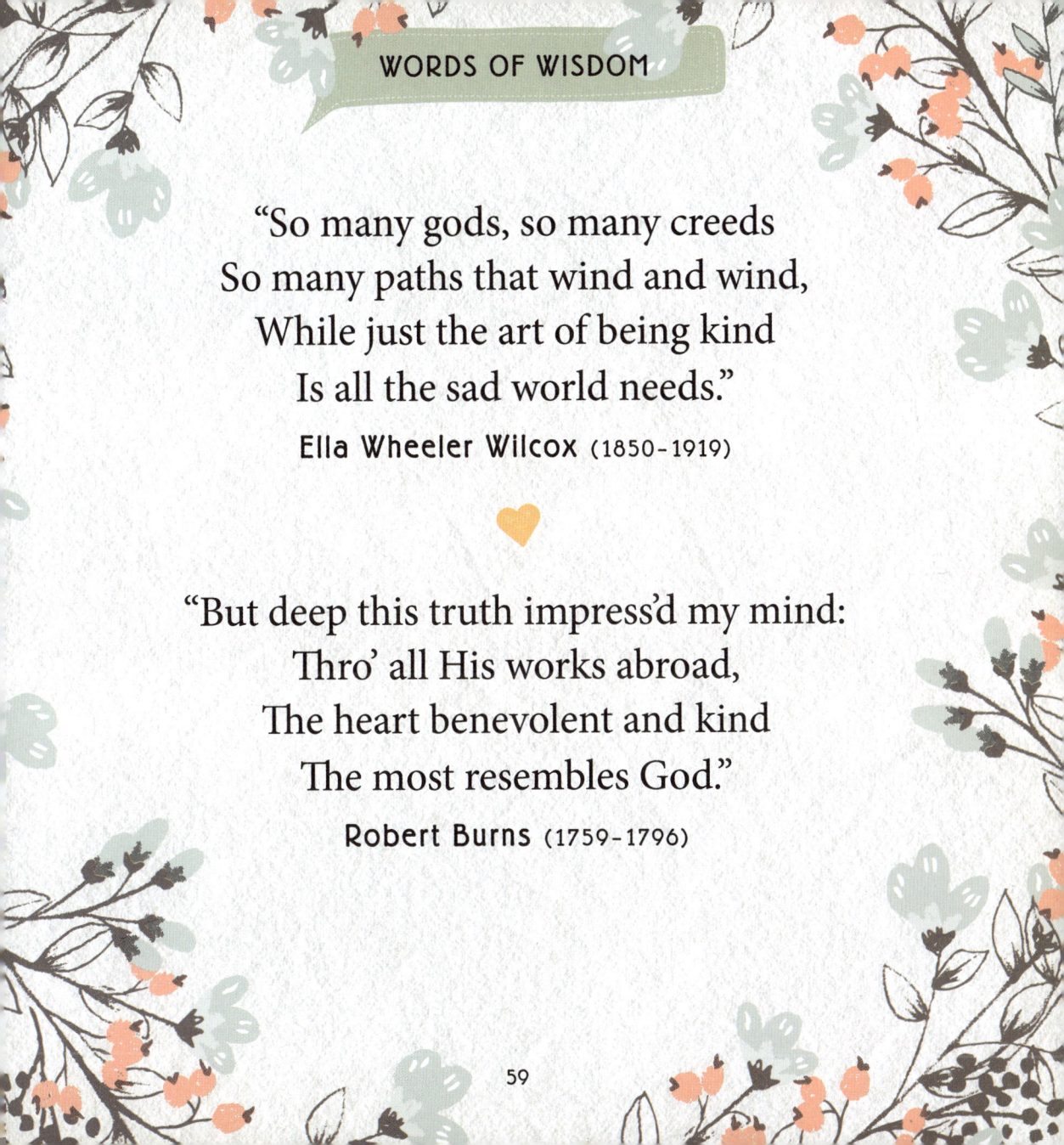

"So many gods, so many creeds
So many paths that wind and wind,
While just the art of being kind
Is all the sad world needs."

Ella Wheeler Wilcox (1850–1919)

"But deep this truth impress'd my mind:
Thro' all His works abroad,
The heart benevolent and kind
The most resembles God."

Robert Burns (1759–1796)

Offset your carbon footprint each time you book a flight.

Help someone who is struggling with their grocery bags.

Read your child a story or offer to go to school to help children with their reading.

"He who allows his day
to pass by without practicing
generosity and enjoying life's
pleasures is like a blacksmith's bellows:
he breathes but does not live."

Indian

"Every man goes down to his
death bearing in his hands only that
which he has given away."

Persian

MILES OF KINDNESS

My neighbors recently gave me a car. They had got a new (used) car so they simply gave me theirs. They asked for nothing in return – they just wanted me to be able to take my two young children to school in comfort, as I'd previously been getting the bus and walking the two-mile round trip.

They truly live by their beliefs and have greatly enhanced my life through their generosity, even though they could have benefitted from having two cars. I hope to one day be in a position to pay this good deed forward.

Crystal R

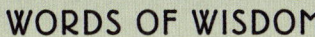
"One kind word can warm
three snowy peaks."

Nigerian

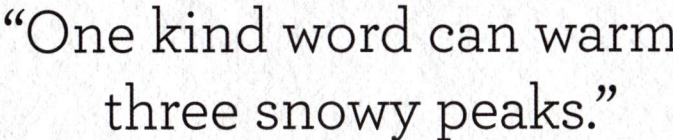

"Kindness can pluck the whiskers of a lion."

Chinese

"A man is judged by his deeds,
not by his words."

English

Put a treat
and a note
in your kids'
lunchboxes or
backpack.

If you have a trolley full of groceries, let the person behind
with a few items in a basket go ahead of you in line.

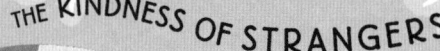
A BAG OF KINDNESS

On New Year's Eve we took a bag packed with a blanket,
a hat, a scarf, gloves, water and biscuits and gave them to a
homeless man we'd seen shivering many times in town. He was
very appreciative and we have seen him recently using the items
we gave him, which is lovely. We will do this now as a tradition
every New Year's.

Marco N.

PICKING UP THE TAB

One day at the local supermarket a lady in front of me couldn't
pay for her groceries after both her credit cards
were refused – I paid her $30 bill for her.

Sam H.

"A bit of fragrance always clings
to the hand that gives roses."

Chinese

Treat a friend to lunch – and not just on a special occasion; do it as a random gesture.

Donate old furniture to a homeless shelter instead of selling it.

Likewise, donate books to schools and good-quality used clothes to shelters or thrift stores.

ACCIDENTS HAPPEN

About ten years ago, I was involved in an accident when I drove into the back of a car. I was really distraught and shaken afterwards but the driver was so kind – he told me it was only a piece of metal and as long as I wasn't hurt it would all be fine. A police car happened to be passing by and the police stopped to help. Together with the driver, they calmed me down, told me what I needed to do and also checked my car to see if it was safe to drive to work. When I got to work I called the insurance company and the shock of it all really hit home so I was in a bit of a state on the phone.

The following morning the doorbell rang and I took a delivery of a huge bunch of flowers. When I read the card I was surprised to see they were from the insurance company. A few months later, I also realized that I'd never been charged the excess on my policy and my premium didn't increase – proof not only in the kindness of strangers but in corporate companies as well!

Karen R.

"That light we see is burning in my hall.
How far that little candle throws his beams!
So shines a good deed in a naughty world."
William Shakespeare (1564–1616)

WORDS OF WISDOM

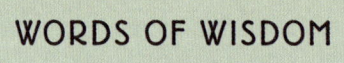

"Kind hearts are the gardens,
Kind thoughts are the roots,
Kind words are the blossoms,
Kind deeds are the fruits."

19th Century rhyme

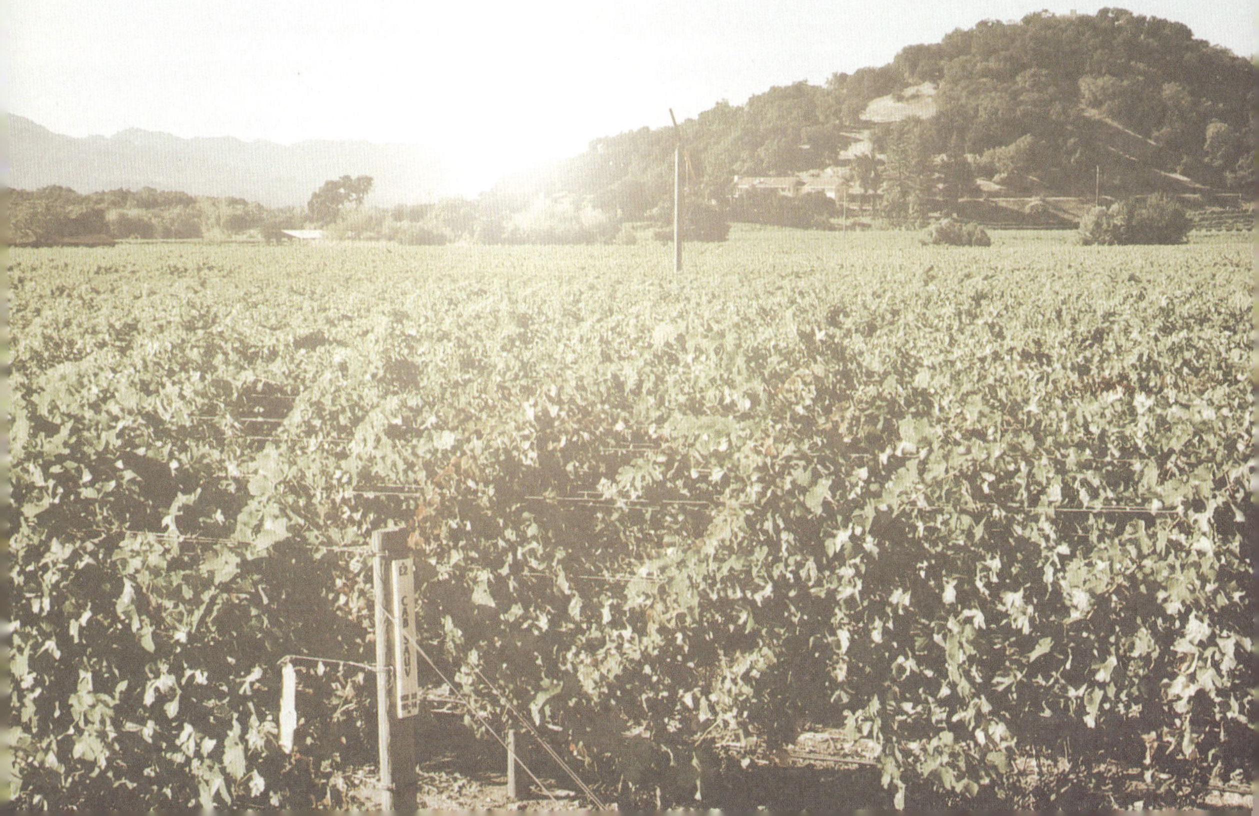

Bricks and mortar

Instead of giving money to charity, why not give your time? Many international organizations are always looking for volunteers to help build schools and medical centers or to work in existing establishments. If you have a particular skill or trade, this is a rewarding way to give something back to society.

Salary sacrifice

Would you really notice if a tiny percentage of your salary was taken from your bank account on the day you got paid? Most people could easily give up just one take-out coffee or sandwich a week, and that's really all it takes to make a difference. Set up a regular payment to your favorite charity and you won't even notice that you're being kind for life.

Invest in education

Set up an annual academic or sports bursary at a local school or college. This could be for a child from a disadvantaged background who wouldn't otherwise get to college, or it could be gifted to your old school for them to choose a recipient.

SMUGGLING CHILDREN TO SURVIVAL

Irena Sendler was born in Warsaw in 1910 and she began helping Jews after the German invasion in 1939. She was part of the Zegota movement (the Council for Aid to Jews) but when the Jewish ghetto was established a year later, Irena found it increasingly difficult to offer assistance to families. Almost half a million Polish Jews were forced to live in the ghetto and it soon became apparent that the area was no more than a holding station before people were transported to concentration camps.

Dressed in nurses' uniforms, Irena and one of her colleagues were able to enter the ghetto and distribute food and medicine. They would then smuggle children out of the ghetto, coming up with ever more ingenious ways to hide them and escape notice – babies and children left the ghetto in everything from suitcases to toolboxes. Once outside the children were given new identities but Irena kept all their original names safely hidden away, hoping that some of those saved would one day be reunited with their parents.

The Nazis eventually discovered Irena's activities and she was imprisoned and tortured. She managed to escape with the help of Zegota; she assumed a new identity and returned to smuggling children to safety. It is believed that Irena saved the lives of 2,500 children during the war.

Put a chocolate on each family member's pillow so they see it when they go to bed.

If you see something that has been dropped on the ground – a purse, a scarf, a cell – be sure to keep it safe until you try and find out who owns it.

Bring a cake into work for your colleagues.

FORGOTTEN FARE

When I was 12, I got the bus into town on my own for the first time. After shopping I realized I'd forgotten to save the bus fare home in the excitement of going out alone. I started crying at the bus stop and an elderly lady gave me the fare – I was so grateful. Then, a few months ago, I was waiting to pay for the gym and a teenage boy in line hadn't brought the right money for his pass. I paid the extra and remembered the old lady from when I was 12.

Sabina D.

If your child can't make a friend's birthday party,
buy the child a gift anyway.

TROLLEY SAVIOR

Recently a lady in the supermarket overheard me tell my son that we would have to go home, as I didn't have a coin for the cart. She came up to me and gave me the money, and told me that someone had done it for her before. It's not a huge thing to do but it meant the world to me at the time.

Megan T.

Put some money or a gift certificate in an envelope and leave it in the mailbox of someone you know living nearby who is struggling financially.

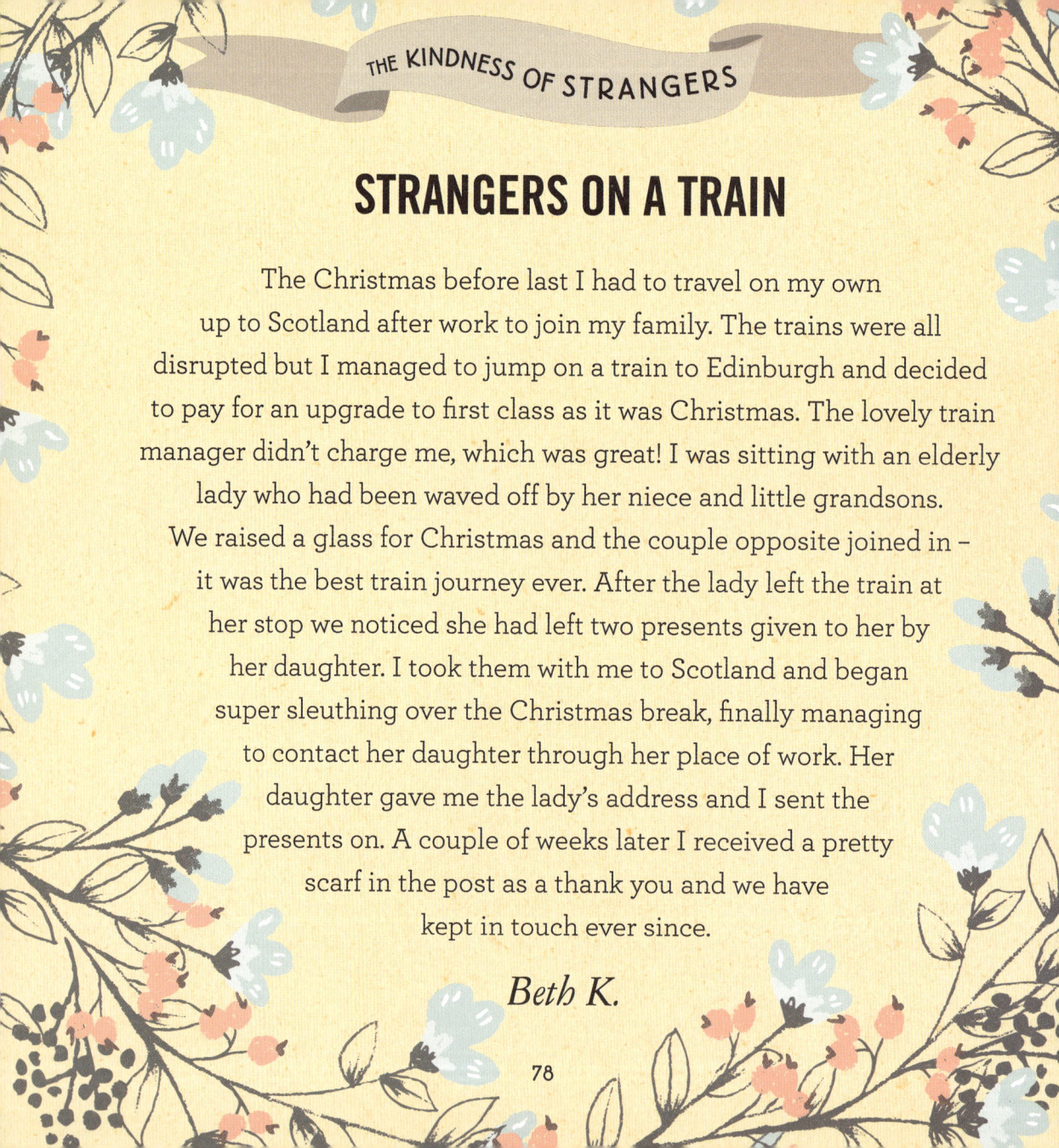

STRANGERS ON A TRAIN

The Christmas before last I had to travel on my own
up to Scotland after work to join my family. The trains were all
disrupted but I managed to jump on a train to Edinburgh and decided
to pay for an upgrade to first class as it was Christmas. The lovely train
manager didn't charge me, which was great! I was sitting with an elderly
lady who had been waved off by her niece and little grandsons.
We raised a glass for Christmas and the couple opposite joined in –
it was the best train journey ever. After the lady left the train at
her stop we noticed she had left two presents given to her by
her daughter. I took them with me to Scotland and began
super sleuthing over the Christmas break, finally managing
to contact her daughter through her place of work. Her
daughter gave me the lady's address and I sent the
presents on. A couple of weeks later I received a pretty
scarf in the post as a thank you and we have
kept in touch ever since.

Beth K.

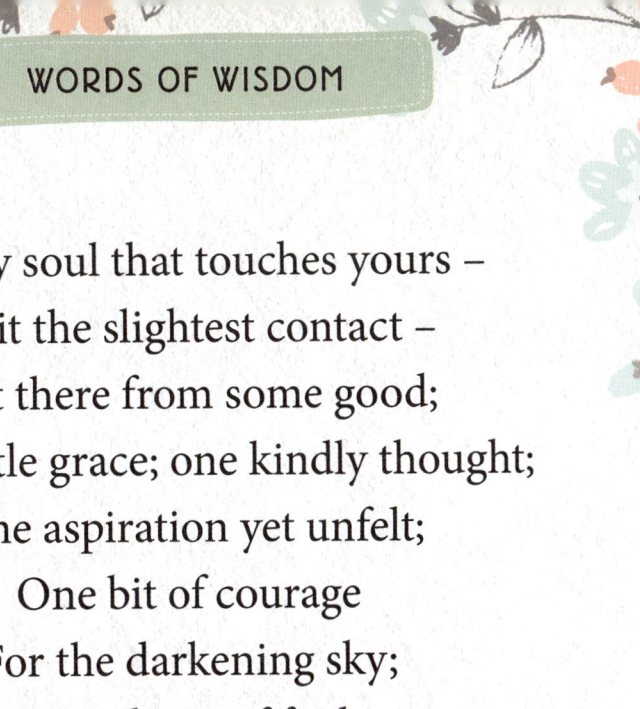

"Every soul that touches yours –
Be it the slightest contact –
Get there from some good;
Some little grace; one kindly thought;
One aspiration yet unfelt;
One bit of courage
For the darkening sky;
One gleam of faith
To brave the thickening ills of life;
One glimpse of brighter skies –
To make this life worthwhile
And heaven a surer heritage."

George Eliot (1819–1880)

"No one is useless in this world who lightens the burdens of another."

Charles Dickens (1812-1870)

"Kindness is the language which the deaf can hear and the blind can see."

Mark Twain (1835-1910)

One can pay back the loan of gold, but one dies forever in debt to those who are kind.

Malayan

Buy coffee and donuts for all your colleagues on the way into work.

Have a movie and pizza night for the kids.

Cook the family's favorite meal.

FEAT OF ENDURANCE

On the night of January 18 1881 a ferocious storm hit the area around Robin Hood's Bay in North Yorkshire. A ship called the *Visitor* foundered off the coast and although there was a local lifeboat, it wasn't up to the task of tackling the gale-force winds and treacherous waves.

As the crew of the *Visitor* struggled to stay on board the doomed ship, a wire was sent to Whitby – a coastal town north of Robin Hood's Bay – to send their more able lifeboat around the coast to save the men. But with the storm worsening, the Whitby crew realized it would be impossible to launch the lifeboat from their position; they would simply be condemning it to the same fate as the *Visitor*.

Eventually, it was decided that the men of Whitby would pull the lifeboat over ground to Robin Hood's Bay – the only problem being that it was a distance of almost six miles. With lives at stake, there was no thought of personal safety as every able-bodied man came out to help.

As the boat was dragged to the bay, more people joined in to help until there were hundreds of volunteers, pushing and pulling the Whitby lifeboat. It took two attempts to reach the stricken ship – the first time the lifeboat was beaten back to shore and half its oars were shattered in the effort. But perseverance paid off and eventually the boat reached the *Visitor*. Every crew member was saved.

Try and do at least one small
act of kindness each day –
life is too short not to.

GOOD DEED DIARY